BETRAYAL TRAUMA: SURVIVAL GUIDE FOR THE FIRST 90 DAYS

Lisa Archinal

BETRAYAL TRAUMA: SURVIVAL GUIDE FOR THE FIRST 90 DAYS

You just found out your partner has cheated on you. First, I am so sorry this has happened to you. I know how this feels and it's devastating. You are now part of a growing club, along with thousands of others, that you never chose to join. Know that as horrible as this is, you are NOT alone. There are communities and resources ready to help with your healing journey.

For today, when this pain and trauma is so fresh, what are the immediate things you need to do? Imagine you've been in a terrible car accident. You were driving along thinking what a beautiful day it is. Traffic is light and there's good music on the radio. All of a sudden, out of nowhere, a mack truck t-bones your car. The airbag deploys but the damage is catastrophic. You're thrown from the car unconscious. After several minutes you wake up. You're disoriented. Where are you? What's happened? Is anyone coming to help me? You need to get to a hospital.

These are common feelings of a betrayed spouse just finding out about their partner's affair. This is known as D-Day (discovery day).

I remember moments of those early days. Disoriented. Weak. Confused. Angry. Hopeless. Where do I start? Who do I call first? What's the first step to address this trauma? I felt like I should be in a hospital with people rushing around me trying to stop the bleeding. But I was alone in my house. My children, thankfully, were teens and would be at school during the day so I was able to, as best I could, process and decide what to do.

By God's grace, my pastor knew about my husband's affair and was a safe and healthy place for me to start. I asked my sister to go with me to meet with him. He had helped others in my situation and he gave me some great advice. The Lord also brought a couple of dear friends who'd been through the same pain and guided me in those early days.

I'm going to share with you eight items to focus on right now that will set you up for success on your healing journey. These are...
1. Create a safe space
2. Choose support for yourself
3. Secure a therapist
4. Accept grief
5. Prioritize your health
6. Identify wise advisors
7. Ask for time off
8. Determine a plan for your kids

As I look at this list and think about how I felt in those first days it can seem overwhelming. There were days it was all I could do to feed myself, much less go through a list of critical things to do. However, these are exactly that - critical.

This list is about YOU. It's for you. It's to care for you. It's highly unlikely anyone is going to come in and do these things for you. This is the time to focus on yourself and this list is your friend. It's going to help you take those first steps after having your legs knocked out from under you.

STEP 1 CREATE A SAFE SPACE

There's an important word you need to learn - BOUNDARIES. I encourage you to learn all you can about this concept. I had no idea what boundaries were when I was hit with this betrayal grenade. Once I began to understand that boundaries were imperative to my recovery, I started to exercise them.

Boundaries may be defined as: What I will or will not do to take care of myself and my responsibilities. A boundary is directly related to what you need to care for yourself. A good example would be: I need you to stay somewhere else for a while so that I can feel safe. A bad example would be: I need you (betrayer) to get counseling.

You can't force your spouse to change or make healthy choices. You can only control you.

When my husband told me about his affair it threw me into a traumatic state. The last thing I wanted was to be near him. I asked him to stay someplace else while I figured out what to do next. I didn't know it yet but I was exercising my first boundary.

I didn't just ask him to leave because I was angry. I was angry but mainly I did not feel emotionally safe around him. Psychologically I needed distance from the person who'd inflicted such pain on me. If you had been physically or sexually assaulted by a stranger, you wouldn't want to stay in the same house with that person. You would set a boundary. Why would staying in the same house with someone who's deeply afflicted you emotionally (which impacts you physically and sexually as well) be good for you either?

Creating physical distance from your spouse is an area where you need to do what is right for you. Everyone's situation is different. It may not be possible for your spouse to leave the house but what about sleeping in another room? Being gone several hours in the day to give you space? The main point I'm making here is that to even begin to start healing you need to speak up for what you need.

You don't have to be nasty, throw things, sling curse words at your spouse in order to say what you need (as a matter of fact, I discourage you from doing that as it only inflates the trauma to yourself). But you do need to speak up for yourself. If you need your husband to stay someplace else even for a few days you can ask him to do that. If he refuses to go, that tells a story and will help you determine if the marriage is worth trying to save.

Another reason for some distance is that there's a very high likelihood that you've only discovered the tip of the iceberg. I'm sorry to tell you that but it's true. You need some time to get the full story. Take a minute and think through your surroundings, what your options are and what boundaries you need so that you can feel safe while you process this crisis.

STEP 2 CHOOSE SUPPORT FOR YOURSELF

Let's go back to the car accident analogy. If you'd been in a serious accident who would you call? Who would come sit by your bed? Who would drive you home when you're discharged from the hospital? Bring you meals? Pick up your meds or run errands for you?

These are your closest inner circle people. Who can you trust with this very delicate, excruciating news? It may be one person for now. Mine was about five girlfriends. For me, this consisted of my big sister, my lifelong best friend, a long time friend who had been through the same experience and was handling it in a mature, healthy way and a couple of other amazing women of faith that I knew would come alongside me and my children. They would pray for me, speak words of hope, listen well, love on my kids and provide practical support as needed.

As painful as it is to tell the story, you must share with these trusted people. This is not a journey to take alone! You've got to have emotional support during this time. The type of friend you're looking for will...
- keep your story private
- sit with you while you cry
- listen with empathy
- not get you worked up with their own emotions or opinions
- protect you by helping you think straight when your emotions are running high
- be willing to run interference with people who are not safe
- make sure you eat and sleep
- love your children well

Even if you have only one of these people thank God you do. As you carefully select who you will trust it's equally important to be aware of who NOT to trust. Imagine you are in intensive care. Do you have a mother-in-law who would come visit you just to say how terrible you look? A neighbor who would bring you flowers only to get dirty details so she could spread rumors of how the accident was your fault?

Friends, think carefully. Your world has just been shattered. You're in a very vulnerable place. Have this view - the ones with whom you choose to share are HONORED to know your story. Who is worthy of walking alongside you? Choose wisely in these early days.

STEP 3 SELECT A THERAPIST

This may be the most important thing you do. It's critical to find the right therapist. There are many to choose from and not all of them will be the right fit. Here are some tips and questions to consider.

What does your insurance cover? See if your insurance covers mental healthcare providers. When you find a therapist you want to work with, ask first if they take your insurance. Many good therapists do not work with insurance so you'll have to file on your end. It's a hassle but you've GOT to get therapy so just buckle up and do it. It will be worth it!

What type of therapist treats betrayal trauma? When looking for a therapist, make certain they have specialized training in betrayal trauma therapy and that they've been working with patients in this area for several years. A good betrayal trauma therapist should have special training/certifications in cognitive behavioral therapy. My therapist also uses [1]EMDR and it's been revolutionary in my healing.

A variety of mental health agencies maintain searchable lists of licensed practitioners in your area. For example, BloomforWomen.com has a list of therapists who are all certified in betrayal trauma therapy.

Questions you may want to ask a prospective therapist:

- What is your counseling experience? How long have you been in practice?
- What types of clients do you work with?
- What are your areas of expertise?
- What is your fee? Do you offer a sliding scale? What is your cancellation policy?
- What's your policy regarding phone calls? Are you reachable in a crisis or an emergency? Do you charge for phone conversations?
- What's your experience working with trauma and abuse? Do you have experience working with PTSD? What modalities do you use? (For example, cognitive-behavioral therapy, EMDR, etc.)

I found my therapist by asking my friend who had been through the same trauma. She loved her therapist so I started there. She was hard to get into and I had to wait several weeks to get in. Once I was in I saw her every week for many months. I urge you to prioritize finding a therapist you feel comfortable with and start treatment as soon as possible.

Another important step related to therapy is finding a support group. There is a wonderful organization called Infidelity Survivors Anonymous (ISA). I absolutely did not want to join a support group at first but my therapist insisted and held me accountable.

Go to isurvivors.org. Find an in person or virtual meeting. When you attend a meeting there will be women who will share their phone numbers for you to reach out to talk to someone who can relate to what you're going through. There will also be women who are willing to sponsor you. I know this is so hard and you're currently drowning in pain but grab this lifeline. Go through the 12 step recovery program. You'll learn some excellent tools to help you heal and meet some amazing women who will give you hope and encouragement.

If this is your first time to experience severe trauma it can be frightening when traumatic responses start to happen. Don't panic. These are expected symptoms and therapy will begin to help you know what to do when they arise. As you begin to heal, these symptoms normally subside and you can actually find you are healthier than you were before this terrible awful thing happened.

So, what does betrayal trauma feel like? Here are some of the symptoms you may experience:
- Overwhelming emotions
- Problems sleeping, falling asleep, staying asleep, sleeping too much
- 'Brain fog,' hard time focusing, memory issues
- Changes in appetite or weight
- Anxiety/panic attacks

- Depression
- Intrusive images/flashbacks
- Difficulty caring for self or others
- Isolation

This is not an **exhaustive** list of symptoms you may experience. Betrayal trauma is complex and can affect everyone differently. Personally, I had varying degrees of all of these. This is where your trusted friends and an excellent therapist are vital.

STEP 4 ACCEPT GRIEF

This is sort of part B of Step 3. It takes time to move through the grieving process. This is not something you can rush. Allow yourself to grieve. My personality type is to suck it up, be strong, and move forward. Ugh. You cannot do that in severe trauma. To actually heal and prevent turning into an all out crazy person, you have to allow yourself to cry and get mad.

If you're a Christian, like I am, maybe you grew up being taught to put on a smile. Good Christians don't get angry. Good Christians don't mourn, or feel sad. That's BULL. Jesus wept! Jesus got angry! The Bible doesn't say not to get angry, it says, 'in your anger, do not sin', Ephesians 4:26.

God made us with all the emotions he himself has. We are made in his image. It's not just okay to feel angry and sad - it's healthy! Now is not the time to stuff your emotions. Allow yourself to grieve. Buy stock in Kleenex and carve out time to process your feelings.

Also, in these first days you may find yourself bursting into tears or suddenly feeling enraged. That's okay. If you're in a public place, try to excuse yourself and try to make it to the bathroom or your car. Sometimes, I had to try hard to distract myself temporarily because I wasn't in a place where I could let my emotions out. That's okay too, just don't stuff them and ignore them.

One of the best gifts I got early on was from my sister. I'm including the link here. She gave me a Dammit Doll. It sounds hilarious and it is - you need humor right now! Get yourself one of these then go where no one can see or hear you. Sometimes I went behind my garage and smacked it against the brick. Sometimes I was in my closet slamming it against the door frame. There will be times when you're so angry you think you're going to explode. This is better! This is a healthy way to get the anger out of you without hurting yourself or someone else.

Grieving comes in waves. You can't control when an emotion will hit but you can choose what to do with it. Remember, feelings are not good or bad. They just 'are'. Now is not the time to judge yourself for how you are feeling. Now is the time to show compassion to yourself. Treat yourself like you would treat your best friend - with love and kindness and space to grieve.

STEP 5 PRIORITIZE YOUR HEALTH

This was an especially hard one for me. Because of my husband's sexual addiction, he put me at serious risk of disease. His infidelity literally could have killed me.

I remember looking up a clinic that did HIV/STD testing with a relatively short turnaround. I was so ashamed walking into the clinic. This is an example of a time when emotions raged. Fear, anger, regret, sadness. It's a lot to handle but so important to make sure you are physically okay. Thankfully, I was not carrying any diseases. As hard as it was to go through that I'm so glad I did and you will be too.

Going through this testing made me aware of my all around physical health and the toll trauma was taking on my body. Another important aspect of experiencing trauma is monitoring your nervous system. Your body is in constant high alert. You need to help yourself move into a state of rest.

I started taking hot baths each night. I'd turn on spa music, light candles, and get a book. It was good for my physical body to be kind of forced into a state of relaxation. I posted scripture by my bed, on my bathroom mirror, etc. to remind me God loves me and He is my healer. I played worship music in my house. Think about what will help bring calm to your racing mind.

I also talked to my doctor. She put me on anti-anxiety medication for several months until my body was able to produce enough serotonin on its own. She also had me take a non-addictive sleep aid because early on I was not sleeping at all which feeds into a vicious cycle of anxiety and depression.

Pro-tip - drink lots of water and do your best to give yourself nourishing meals. You may not realize how hard your body is working when in trauma.

It's important to remember we are not one dimensional beings. We are emotional, physical, mental, social, intellectual, and spiritual creatures. We must address our entire selves! Take care of your body. It's fighting hard on your behalf.

STEP 6 IDENTIFY WISE ADVISORS

I just shared how we are whole beings with multiple dimensions. I've mentioned social, emotional, mental and physical. I want to talk now about the intellectual dimension.

You're in a whole new world now whether you accept it or not. The smartest thing you can do is accept it and start learning.

I'll share a list of readings later. First, I need to tell you another hard truth you need to face. Your marriage might end now, later, or be saved. In the first 90 days after betrayal you need to assume the worst for your own protection.

Call a good attorney and know your rights. A good attorney is expensive. If you cannot afford an attorney there are resources for free legal advice. The American Bar Association offers pro bono services for those who qualify.

Partition Agreement. This is a term I had never heard and I want to share it with you because it could be a game changer depending on your husband's willingness to seek recovery and reconcile the marriage. In my case, my husband desperately wanted to save our marriage and our family. I found a good attorney through a reference from a friend. When I met with the attorney he said Texas was a no fault state and everything would be split 50/50 for the most part. This wasn't acceptable to me. I asked what else could be done and the attorney introduced me to the term Partition Agreement.

A Partition Agreement is where one spouse can legally sign over all their assets to the other spouse. I jumped on that like butter on a biscuit. I got all of our financial investment accounts and my husband, because he was anxious to prove his devotion, signed the agreement. All of his investments are now in my name. This is BIG.

Here's the thing. I'm not out to be cruel or harsh. I was in survival mode and this was a life saver. I had been a stay at home mom most of our marriage and now work for a non-profit. I would have been in trouble if he'd left me with 50/50. This financial security allowed me to relax in this one area and focus on my emotional healing. It also was a big test to see how seriously my husband was taking reconciliation.

Your husband may not be willing to do this. Not many are. The point is for you to know all your options. I had never heard of this term. I just kept asking questions and learned about it. Keep pressing your resources to learn as much as you can about how to protect yourself.

Next, open a bank account solely in your name that your spouse is unaware of. Another step I took immediately after learning about my husband's betrayal was calling our bank and opening a private account. I then moved money from our joint account to this private account. This is where you need to think through your own situation, what you want and what consequences could arise. If your husband is not wanting to reconcile, if he's cruel, etc, ask for advice from a trusted advisor or attorney before taking this step.

Another tip is to start taking out small amounts of cash every time you go to the store and begin to build an emergency fund.

Know passwords to joint accounts. If you have a financial planner you've worked with, call him/her and ask for advice on protecting yourself. If you're not sure this person will remain confidential, find another financial expert and know your rights.

Okay, here's my book list. I'm sure there are other great ones and you may start one of these and find it doesn't meet your needs but these are some that helped me in the start of my journey.

- Redeeming Heartache - Allender/Loerzel
- The Language of Letting Go - Beattle
- Moving Beyond Betrayal - Tidwell Palmer
- Torn Asunder - Carder
- It's Not Supposed to Be This Way - Terkeurst
- Forgiving What You Can't Forget - Terkeurst
- Hope After Betrayal - Wilson
- Your Sexually Addicted Spouse - Steffens/Means
- Stop Sex Addiction - Magness

- Mending a Shattered Heart - Carnes
- Thriving Despite a Difficult Marriage - Misja
- Facing Heartbreak - Carnes/Lee/Rodriguez

I didn't put this on the above list but I have to talk about it - the Bible. I don't know what I would have done without God's Word to remind me of who God is, that He loves me perfectly and unconditionally, that bad things happen but God is still good and trustworthy.

STEP 7 ASK FOR TIME OFF

Grieving, counseling, attending to financial affairs, caring for your children, etc. all takes time. In the early days I could barely get my kids up and out the door for school before I collapsed on the couch. I let my employer know we'd had a crisis in our family and may need some time off. Fortunately, I work for a supportive organization who gave me some level of flexibility.

If you have younger kids, now is a great time to ask grandparents or trusted friends to take your kids for a few hours here and there to give you time to process as well as to have adults other than yourself loving on your kids. Be careful not to isolate yourself but it is okay to have a few hours here and there to just cry, think through next steps, read or go get a massage.

I was able to get a massage membership at a place like Massage Heights. Again, my friend who had been through the same experience told me it's so important to take time to do things that help regulate your nervous system. Getting a monthly massage (at a reasonable price) was a big help to me and a good use of time.

Think about this question: how can you use one hour of your time to bring healing to your soul? Is it going for a walk in the sun? Taking a hot bath? Watching a funny show? Cuddling with your dog? People cannot read your mind. Talk to your boss and/or other organizations where you have commitments. Ask for what you need and be intentional to make time to heal.

STEP 8 DETERMINE A PLAN FOR THE KIDS

Thinking about your children learning this awful truth is hard. If you're like me you'd do anything to protect your kids. One of the biggest sources of rage for me through this journey is thinking about how my kids have been crushed by what their father did.

My husband and I took a few weeks to figure out what to tell (and not tell) our children who were teens at the time. We prayed a lot about it. We sought wise counsel from our pastor whom we respected as well as a therapist.

Open and honest communication is essential when helping children navigate the impact of infidelity. If they haven't discovered the affair and depending on circumstances, it may not be necessary to tell them.

Here are some tips for parents if your child has discovered or needs to be told about an affair:

- Age-Appropriate Conversations: Tailor your discussions to your child's age and maturity level. Use age-appropriate language and provide as much information as they can handle.
- Create a Safe Space: Ensure that your child feels safe expressing their feelings and concerns without fear of judgment or retaliation.
- Be Transparent: They don't need details about the parental infidelity. They only need to know how it impacts them. In our case, they had to be told something as I had asked my husband not to live at home for a season.
- Reassure Love and Support: Emphasize that your love for them remains unwavering, regardless of the challenges within the relationship.
- Avoid blaming the other parent: This is an adult issue and the child shouldn't become a caregiver for either of the parents.

In many cases, the emotional impact of infidelity on children can be so profound that it requires professional intervention. Child therapists and counselors can provide valuable guidance and support for children trying to process their emotions. Additionally, family therapy can be an effective way to address the broader family dynamics and facilitate healing.

Before we told our kids we looked into therapists our kids might want to go meet with to help them with their own trauma. We wanted to be ready with some resources for them. They had good relationships with trusted youth pastors and mentors so we let those folks know ahead of time so they could be ready to receive our kids. We planned the conversation on a weekend when there wasn't a lot going on and our kids could have space to begin to process and work through their own grief.

Children may have difficulty processing their feelings about their parents' infidelity. Encourage them to express themselves in healthy ways, such as through art, journaling, or talking to a trusted friend or family member. Emphasize that it's normal to feel a wide range of emotions and that their feelings are valid.

I highly encourage you to prayerfully think through what is appropriate to tell or not tell your children. Above all, NEVER use your children as leverage to hurt your spouse or to be a crutch for you. If you choose to walk through your trauma in a healthy manner you can really help your children to get through this valley and come out on the other side actually being emotionally and mentally healthy and stable. It takes a lot of work and wisdom but it can be done.

CONCLUSION

As counter-intuitive as it sounds, the best thing you can do beginning now to keep hope alive is to focus on yourself.

When you practice good **self-compassion, yo**u will be much more capable of navigating the challenging journey you're on. You will feel better, and when you feel better you will be more prepared to face the ultimate outcome of your situation—whether your relationship survives infidelity or it doesn't.
Self-care is like wearing a seat belt. Loving and accepting yourself protects you from being devastated or completely losing hope because your purpose, joy and happiness were based on another person showing up for you in just the way you want or never letting you down. Our life cannot be based on someone else. I know this is hard!

I encourage you to take these first 90 days to focus on yourself. Get these eight areas going. Focus on your health and on finding out all of the truth about your spouses failing. You can notice and acknowledge the progress of your spouse, which is also another source of hope. But first, you must create ways to love and honor yourself in the same ways you want others to love and honor you. There is hope!

---

[1]Eye Movement Desensitization and Reprocessing
https://revelationcounselingblog.wordpress.com/2023/02/24/ten-benefits-of-emdr-therapy/

Printed in Great Britain
by Amazon